I can only imagine
     what it will be like when I walk by your side
I can only imagine
     what my eyes will see when your face is before me

Surrounded by your glory what will my heart feel?
Will I dance for you Jesus or in awe of you be still?
Will I stand in your presence or to my knees will I fall?
Will I sing hallelujah? Will I be able to speak at all?

I can only imagine
     when that day comes when I find myself standing in the Son
I can only imagine
     when all I will do is forever, forever worship you . . .

I can only imagine.

I Can Only Imagine™

STORIES OF ETERNAL HOPE

MercyMe

with Wendy Lee Nentwig

COUNTRYMAN

Nashville, Tennessee

I Can Only Imagine™

Copyright © 2004 by Simpleville Music, Inc.

Published by the J. Countryman® division of the Thomas Nelson Book
Group, Nashville, Tennessee 37214

The New King James Version of the Bible (NKJV), copyright © 1979,
1980, 1982, 1992, Thomas Nelson, Inc., Publishers. Used by permission.

J. Countryman® is a trademark of Thomas Nelson Inc.

I CAN ONLY IMAGINE is a trademark of Simpleville Music, Inc.

Project Editor: Kathy Baker

Designed by Koechel Peterson & Associates, Minneapolis, MN

MercyMe photos by David & Luke Edmonson.
    Additional band photography by Eric Welch.

ISBN 1-4041-0177-2

Printed and bound in the United States of America

www.thomasnelson.com
www.jcountryman.com

IMAGINATION IS A POWERFUL THING. We can choose either to call up images of comfort or to dream up dreadful scenarios. Often, we employ it in an attempt to answer that consuming question, "What if . . . ?" We can be held hostage by our imaginations or use them to draw closer to God. The choice is ours.

Whatever is true, whatever is noble,
whatever is right, whatever is pure,
whatever is lovely, whatever is admirable—
if anything is excellent or praiseworthy—
think about such things.
PHILIPPIANS 4:8

"I can only imagine."

They were just four simple words. A phrase I scribbled in notebooks and on scraps of paper in the months after my father died, trying to make sense of an unimaginable loss. I was still in my teens when cancer took my dad from me, and the well-meaning words of others—"he's in a better place" or "he wouldn't want to be back here"—did little to comfort me.

Years later I would stumble upon that phrase and, still hurting, I would turn it into a song in an attempt to help myself heal. In the beginning, I wasn't trying to imagine what Heaven was like out of some Christian sense of wonder. I simply was trying to make sense of my father's early death. I had heard all the stories about how wonderful the next life would be, but I was still grieving, struggling to figure out what could be so wonderful about Heaven that my dad would be willing to leave me so soon.

And the song did help. Dad had been a godly man, and imagining my earthly father meeting his heavenly Father helped me heal. Pondering what he was seeing and knowing he was free of the physical limitations he'd had here on earth helped bring me peace. "I Can Only Imagine" seemed to help others who were hurting as well. So while it didn't necessarily fit on the worship album we were recording at the time, MercyMe began to perform the song at every live show.

Even with the positive response, though, my bandmates and I had no idea then how God planned to use that song or how, a decade after his death, it would help my father fulfill a promise he made to continue to take care of me.

We could see the impact the song was having on others by the expressions on their faces when we sang it each night. Afterward, they lined up to share their stories. At times it was overwhelming, looking at their photos of lost loved ones, seeing their pain and grief, and hearing how the song had been played at a funeral or memorial service. Some nights the band would return to the bus, and we would just break down.

Although each person's story was unique, there were many common threads. After hearing hundreds of tales, I began to anticipate them, to prepare myself for another emotional story. But just when I thought I knew what was coming, I would be surprised. One man came through the line after a show, his three sons in tow. As he began to tell of losing his wife, I nodded in understanding. But as I began to offer my condolences, the father stopped me. "That's not what I wanted to tell you," he insisted. Then he went on to share how all three of his sons had accepted

Christ that night. They had only agreed to come to the show because they wanted to hear "I Can Only Imagine," one of their mother's favorite songs, and they left with their lives and hearts changed.

God continued to use the song in my own life as well. Before he died, my father set up an annuity, which ensured I would receive a check every month for ten years. It wasn't enough to go crazy, but it allowed me to work on my music without having to deliver pizzas on the side. Even though the money would only arrive for a set amount of time, my father promised me before he died that he would still provide for me after that ten years was up. As a teenager, you don't want to think about a parent dying, let alone what will happen after, so I kind of blew him off and didn't give much thought to what he said.

In January 2002, "I Can Only Imagine" was running up the charts. I had been watching its progress with interest, waiting to see if it would land in the number one spot. But then my son was born, and the charts faded from my mind. Not until I was doing a radio interview did I find out "I Can Only Imagine" had reached the top spot. As the DJ congratulated me, I was overcome with emotion—but not because my song was a success. A bigger story was unfolding.

The last check from Dad had just arrived, and that money, still a good chunk of my growing family's income, would be missed. But as the DJ gave me the news, understanding began to dawn. My father's words came back to me: "Even when the money runs out, I'll still be taking care of you." And he was! The song he had inspired was going to keep the promise my dad had made all those years before.

As the months flew by, it became clear that this little song was doing more than putting to rest lost loved ones; it was changing the lives of the living. And no one was more amazed than me. God was taking this song to places we couldn't have dreamed. Mainstream radio began playing it, and calls flooded into the stations. This overt message of faith was resonating with people who hadn't considered spiritual matters in years. Others told of being so moved they had to pull over to the side of the road until the song was done playing.

The response was beyond MercyMe's comprehension, but we knew that ultimately it wasn't about us or even about this song—God was using a willing band and a simple tune about Heaven to draw people to Himself.

And He's not done yet.

"That which dominates our imagination and our thoughts will determine our lives and our character."

RALPH WALDO EMERSON

I WAS FIRST INTRODUCED to "I Can Only Imagine" in February 2001. I was looking for a song to sing for a church coffeehouse when my friend told me about it. He bragged on and on about how awesome the lyrics were. He became famous for his passion for this song and it became "his" song. He would wonder and wonder about what it would be like to go to Heaven and see Christ.

It is that song that has helped me mourn his death.

On the morning of September 11, 2001, on the 93rd floor of the North Tower of the World Trade Center, Andy J. Kim stopped wondering. Andy's death, though tragic and untimely (he was only 27), reminds me of the promise that we have in Christ that we will one day be "surrounded by His glory."

RICHARD J. LEE

My 9-year-old brother, Hunter, died of myocarditis in October 2002. It is a rare virus that attacks the heart and can cause sudden death in children. He attended a football game, happy and healthy, on October 1, and on October 2 he was in a coma. He died eight days later. According to the doctors, he shouldn't have been able to be revived after his heart stopped on October 1, but God knew that we needed those nine days to prepare. Although we wonder why, we can't question God's purpose. We are only left to trust that He knows best.

Hunter was an artist. The picture he drew most was of someone going up to Heaven. He was spoken for.

LEIGHANNE AUSTIN

Humble Beginnings . . .

The first time I heard "I Can Only Imagine," we were driving down the road trying to come up with an arrangement. It was midnight and our old bus had mattresses on the floor, no heat and no air. The song didn't really leave an impression then because I was trying to butcher it, making it up-tempo. Then in 1999, we were packing up in a Sunday school room where we'd been recording, and Jim just kind of came up with that intro while messing around on his piano. Then Bart sat down and finished the song. We had to set all our equipment back up to finish it out. We knew it was important.

MIKE SCHEUCHZER, MercyMe

We were all crammed into one end of the hallway, and Robby was on drums in another room. We just laid it down, and it didn't really take very long. After we were done we just looked at each other and knew it was special.

Nathan Cochran, MercyMe

It's a really simple song, musically.
It's just three chords on the verse and chorus.
The fourth chord doesn't even come
in until the end.
JIM BRYSON
MercyMe

It was originally put on an indie worship record of ours. "I Can Only Imagine" was kind of like a B-side because it didn't fit. It wasn't the traditional verse and chorus. We didn't even play it for several months after we recorded it.
BART MILLARD, MercyMe

I didn't know what we had until we played it for people live. When we played it the first time, half the crowd was crying. That's when I saw the difference in the song.
Robby Shaffer, *MercyMe*

Maybe God gave us imaginations because He knew how much we would need them. On those difficult days when nothing goes right, on those dark nights when it seems like dawn will never come…being able to imagine better times ahead is a gift! Imagination can make all the difference.

Every good and perfect gift is from above . . .

JAMES 1:17

The song "I Can Only Imagine" always helps me think of all the good times and the things God has done for me. When I hear those lyrics, I imagine what I will see when Jesus comes and brings us home to Heaven. I love that song!

Emily Borkowski

So often in life, we adults get consumed by the details of life. Driving here and there, radio going, kids chattering, and taking that occasional work call on the cell. All in a day…

Then "I Can Only Imagine" came on the radio and my seven-year-old daughter started belting it out in the car. She had never heard it before, but it just seemed to come to her. I just sat in awe. She sooo gets it!

LAURIE BURNS

I was driving to work one morning about a year ago and I was pretty depressed. I was going through a divorce and I was in the deepest of places, just carrying on for my children. "I Can Only Imagine" came on the radio and my three-year-old announced, "that's my favorite song." She made me listen to the words, and I sat there and cried. Even though I was so low, God had carried me through, and He was telling me that everything would be fine in the end.

Today, whenever we hear that song, I think of how far I have come because of God speaking to me through my daughter.

Tricia A. Blum-Boeck

Simple Song...Huge Response

This song is inspiring people in ways we never would have thought of. There's a girl named Cheyenne in West Texas. Due to a debilitating disease, she struggles to even walk, but she barrel races her horses and competes in beauty pageants where she does sign language to "I Can Only Imagine." She's a light in her community, and she talks about imagining one day when she can walk again. It's an incredible story of her strength.

MIKE SCHEUCHZER, MercyMe

We hear a ton of different stories on a daily basis. You almost want to desensitize yourself after a while. But that's a wonderful burden to bear.

NATHAN COCHRAN, MercyMe

We were at a radio station in Abilene, Texas, shortly after the song came out, and the DJs were telling us about a high school student who had been killed in a bike accident. Apparently, the song had made such an impact on him as an individual that his parents had the chorus engraved on his tombstone. What a great witness to have. How many people are going to walk through a graveyard and see that?

Robby Shaffer, MercyMe

As chaplain for the UT Arlington baseball team, I traveled with them, leading Bible studies and pre-game devotions. On one long bus ride, I heard one of our tough guy pitchers sing (kind of) the phrase "I can only imagine." I turned around and asked him about it. He said it was the greatest song ever. It just so happened that I had a copy of your *Worship Project* CD with me, and he wanted to hear all of it. Then others wanted to hear. Throughout the road trip, MercyMe CDs were passed up and down the aisle of the bus. One relief pitcher listened to it before every game that weekend. I gave him the CD. I don't think he is a believer, but he has now heard the message clearly through chapel times and your music.

This process has continued for many years now, and I never travel without several MercyMe CDs. I don't know how many I have given away. I have played "I Can Only Imagine" for people in Vietnam, Bosnia, Zimbabwe, and many other countries. I even had the opportunity recently to play the song for people in Afghanistan where music has been banned by the Taliban for more than ten years. There are places where Christian literature is not allowed, but it was so easy to take in your CDs. God is using your gift everywhere. This year I saw a worship/dance team in Campo Grande, Brazil, using "I Can Only Imagine" to share in schools all around their city. All they had was a cassette of the song they had received from a missionary.

We can't imagine what it will be like to meet Jesus face to face in heaven, and we can't imagine the amazing ways He will use us while we are still here. Thank you for your friendship. It has been a privilege to watch God grow and use you all these years. We'll still be praying for the harvest.

Dr. Courtney Cash

Getting Personal . . .

I've lost a few people in the past few months. We always take December and January off. During that time in 2003–2004, I had eight people pass away in just five or six weeks. My wife's only brother was killed in a car accident. He was 20.

There are some nights where it eats you alive. We have nights when we can't take it anymore, but it's not really us handling it in the first place. And we asked for this. There was a day, a long time ago, when we said, "God, use us in any way possible."

BART MILLARD, *MercyMe*

I've lost close loved ones and my own father
has come quite close to death several times.
He's had two strokes and a heart attack.
So when people tell me their stories,
I go there with them. That's all you can do—
go there with them.
Barry Graul, MercyMe

MY MOM HAD BATTLED CANCER five times since 1982. In 2001, they found a tumor on her liver and her intestines were blocked. She couldn't eat so she wasn't strong enough for surgery. When the doctor was telling her this, I remember I was on the edge of the bed. She had some tears, but she said, "I'm tired and I'm just ready to go home."

We took her home on Wednesday, and by Thursday evening she was in a coma. She was comfortable and sedated. Still, she had requested that MercyMe's songs be played all the time. She had always been fascinated by Heaven and by far, her favorite song was "I Can Only Imagine." We had a five–disc changer and with our new CD and our independent releases, there were about seventy songs to choose from. And yet when she took her last breath, "I Can Only Imagine" was playing. I think it was God's way of saying, "She's fine. It's all okay."

My mom was 77 when she passed away, and here's this rock music playing in the background.

Throughout her long struggle with cancer, my mom made it her mission to send a handwritten note to anyone who she found out had the disease. She sent out anywhere from eight thousand to ten thousand letters. She even wrote to President Reagan and heard back from him. The summer before Mom passed away, I sent out an e–mail to our newsletter subscribers asking them to write to my mom if they had a minute. Within a few days, she was getting fifty letters a day. I think the final tally was eight hundred handwritten letters and the same number of e–mail messages. I still have all of them. The highlight of her day was watching for the postman. She would wait for those just like it was Christmas and she was a little kid.

JIM BRYSON, *MercyMe*

Mr. Jim,

I am sorry about your mommy. I know how you feel. But our mommies are in Heaven, and maybe they are friends like me and my friend Mackenzie. I play your song all day long. It makes me happy.

Your friend, Ashley Nicole Liles

My only child, Cameron, was diagnosed in December 2000 with a rare form of childhood cancer. Although he is my hero and fought a great fight against the disease, he went home to Jesus and now has a heavenly birthday, April 21, 2002. "I Can Only Imagine" was a huge comfort to us when Cameron passed away. It also reminds us that in the scope of eternity, this life is just a blip on the radar screen, and we have so much to look forward to when we will be "surrounded by His glory."

KRIS KERWIN

On April 5 of 2002, my nephew, Matthew, was born. He was three months premature. For three wonderful weeks my family and I sang "Jesus Loves Me" to him in the neonatal intensive care unit of Cooks Children's Hospital. As I sang to Matthew each day I would pray over him. My brother and sister-in-law had been trying for years to get pregnant, and Matthew was a miracle from the Lord. I could not conceive that God would take him back from us. However, on April 26th, just three weeks later, that is what God did.

I went into a complete spiritual tailspin. I told my husband there was not a God. I completely shut down. At Matthew's funeral, I watched in agony as my brother and sister-in-law grieved for their baby. I listened to a letter my brother had written to the congregation. The letter said that their faith had been strengthened through these circumstances. I could not fathom that. Then, a guest musician got up to perform. He had come there for a youth retreat, and he told of how he had put the sheet music to "I Can Only Imagine" into his briefcase, not knowing why.

He began the chords to "I Can Only Imagine," and for the first time since Matthew's death something broke through to me. **God spoke to me through that song.** He encouraged me and began the healing process.

It has not been easy. I still miss my nephew. But I can hear that song and know that Matthew is in the arms of Jesus. I know that even after all my seminary classes and degrees, I don't have a clue what Heaven is like, but my nephew does. He doesn't have to imagine anymore. I can't wait for him to show me around.

Angie Bailey

My mom passed away after a lengthy battle with cancer in 1995. I've always felt at peace at her passing, but I wanted her around for my own selfish needs. ("Mom, how long do you cook this turkey?" "Mom, the baby has a fever of 101 degrees. Should I call the doctor?") I'd always tried to envision her up in Heaven, singing in the choir, teaching the Sunday school children, talking and laughing with the angels and with our Lord. But after hearing "I Can Only Imagine" I felt even greater confidence at my mom's presence in Heaven and greater comfort that she was needed elsewhere. She spent her whole life working toward Heaven and getting her whole family there. I know she's where she belongs.

Terry Sommers

I work at my church and a little over a year ago my friend Gary, a member of our worship team, suddenly passed away. It was my job to oversee the worship team as well as the funeral. As I was talking with the pastor about the wishes of the family, he showed me the list of songs that my friend's wife wanted: one was a familiar hymn and the other was "I Can Only Imagine." After the funeral, Gary's wife said what a perfect song this was for Gary, but she did not remember requesting it. She had not even heard it before!

I believe God orchestrated the whole thing. He wanted this song to comfort, encourage, and remind us of what we have to look forward to when we leave this life.

JULIE KLOSIEWSKI

This last year has set my mind and my heart on Heaven like never before. Losing three precious little ones through miscarriage and trying to deal with the pain associated with this loss has me trying to imagine my little ones with Jesus and what it will be like when one day I am able to hold them in my arms. I can't help but feel hope and anticipation of that day. This life is just a small part of the big picture.

Jennifer Parsons

The young mother of a boy on my son's baseball team died unexpectedly. I was so sad and thought about this situation so much that I started grieving my own life. What would my children and my husband do without me? How would I die? Would it hurt? Would I know? Would I miss my family so much?

I really love my life here on Earth. I appreciate everything God has given me. Then it hit me: God has given me these things here on Earth; imagine what is in store for me in Heaven!

MICHELLE M. WEBER

I am forty years old and in today's terms have what would be called ADHD (Attention Deficit Hyperactivity Disorder). When I hear "I Can Only Imagine" there is no doubt in my mind what I will do—I will be still and stand in awe. Many people who know me would probably disagree, but those who know my heart would believe that.

Susan Pralle

38

The first time I heard this song,
I had been going through a period of
doubt, not in my faith, but in what
would keep me "occupied" for eternity.
I know I want to be in the presence
of Jesus, but what could I possibly
do in eternity? Then I realized that
I will do in eternity what I do now—
worship God in all I do.

Carrie Schneider

We get so busy in our lives that it's nice to remember that this isn't the final destination. It's hard for me to imagine a world without burdens, large and small…socks that don't match, bombings in Israel, appointments to keep, World Trade Center attacks, phones ringing, peace in Iraq so our soldiers can come home, what's for dinner? Burdens won't end, but we have a promise of eternal life. I do like to stop and try to imagine what it will be like.

MARY CULLINAN

I Can Only Imagine

My sister, Sarah, passed away on Feb. 20, 2002, four days before her 17th birthday. While Sarah and I have a personal relationship with Jesus Christ, the majority of my family does not. We played "I Can Only Imagine" at her funeral to show everyone a little bit of what Heaven's like and where Sarah now finds her Home, the place she has dreamed of ever since she became a Christian. My dad, Tom, has accepted Jesus into His life as a result of this, and knowing that Sarah is in Heaven with her loving Father has given him and myself a tremendous peace. I just wanted to thank you so much for writing a song that has given people who may not read His Word a glimpse of Heaven and the glory that Sarah lives in now and that the rest of us can experience.

Nikki Baughman

When I first heard this song, I was at a low point in my life. Spiritually, emotionally, and physically drained. When it came on the radio I had to stop the car, I started to cry so hard. Needless to say, "I Can Only Imagine" started me on a path to recovery. I came to Christ after many, many hurts, pains, and abuses. What keeps me going forward is knowing that one day I will be in His mighty and heavenly presence.

MARGIE PERALTA

FEBRUARY 2004

Hi. This is Lt. Col. Joseph Piek, and I'm writing to you from Mosul, Iraq. I deployed in early November from Fort Lewis, Washington, with 3rd Brigade, 2nd Infantry Division, the U.S. Army's first Stryker Brigade Combat Team.

Before I deployed, I became a huge fan of MercyMe's "I Can Only Imagine," just like hundreds of thousands of other people across the U.S. and elsewhere. I'd overplayed the Christian CDs I brought with me, and just last week I bought a MercyMe CD with "I Can Only Imagine." Our Brigade Chaplain, Major Wayne Garcia, and I walk around our compound at night singing this song.

A few nights ago, we lost our first soldier to hostile fire—an improvised explosive device, or IED as they've become known. A friend of the soldier who died sought me out right after the incident. We talked and prayed, and comforted each other. When I finally got to my bunk that night, I played "I Can Only Imagine" until the batteries ran out in my CD player.

I'm sure this song has brought comfort and healing to thousands of people, and this past Monday night, Feb. 16, it brought great comfort to me.

God Bless. Doing my best to witness to our soldiers here in Iraq,

Lt. Col. Joseph Piek
Task Force Olympia Public Affairs Officer / Mosul, Iraq

I've been meaning to get a note off to you for a couple of weeks, but as you can imagine we've been really busy here in Mosul, Iraq. The boxes of CDs that you sent to us in Mosul arrived about two weeks ago, and we've begun distributing these to our soldiers. In distributing them, it has given me an opportunity to tell my story of how Bart's "I Can Only Imagine" touched me. The CDs have brightened many soldiers' spirits. Thank you so much. Keep all our soldiers—as well as the good Iraqi people here who are doing their best to move this country forward—in your prayers.

Thanks,
Lt. Col. Joe Piek
Task Force Olympia Public Affairs / Mosul, Iraq

Beyond Expectations . . .

*I think the song has evolved. The first few years were
for me, to help me heal. Now it's for everyone else.*
Bart Millard, MercyMe

WE LOOK AT THE SONG'S ROLE IN OUR SHOWS AS A GREAT
WITNESSING TOOL. IF IT LETS US GET OUR FOOT IN THE DOOR
WITH PEOPLE, WE'LL PLAY IT THREE TIMES A NIGHT.
ROBBY SHAFFER, MERCYME

When I first met the band, I thought it was
weird that people worshiped to that song.
Now after playing it night after night and
worshiping to it myself, it's a worship song
for me as well. I've cried a hundred times
while playing it. And it's unbelievable to
look out into the audience. You can almost
see the stories behind the faces.
BARRY GRAUL, MercyMe

It's a song that gives hope to people and ultimately points them to Christ.

NATHAN COCHRAN
MercyMe

This song was originally about trying to figure out Heaven, but it's also a question for life. The themes could apply to Heaven, to our lives, or even to worship. Everything I talked about in the song, I've gone through here on Earth—I've danced for joy, I've fallen to the ground—but through it all, I've continued to remain surrounded in His glory.

Bart Millard, MercyMe

As we move from day to day struggling with the cares of our lives, it's hard to imagine that many people struggle even more than we do. People in some other countries deal with war, famine, death, etc. But as Christians, we all have the same hope: Christ. He opened the doors of Heaven for all who would accept Him.

Cynthia Louise Ratliff

This song keeps me grounded. It is a great reminder of the God I love and who also loves me. It helps me to keep perspective of what is important and how I should prioritize things in my life. After all, nothing should be more important than my walk with the Lord. This song brings strength to me because no matter how much fear and negativity there is in this world, a place of peace and everlasting happiness is waiting for me.

JAMIE MOSLEY

I was driving my kids to school, and it was an unusually quiet morning in the car considering I had four kids, ages ten, eight, six, and four. The song "I Can Only Imagine" came on the radio, and I could hear all the kids singing. Even my four-year-old knew all the words. When the song was over, my son asked, "What will Heaven be like?" This started a conversation about God's promises. When I dropped the kids off, I felt so blessed to have had the opportunity to share Jesus with them that morning. I believe that conversation will never be forgotten.

Jennifer A. Larson

I used to think that Heaven was some sort of "state of mind," but then it just hit me: Wow! I will one day be in this actual place where I will see Jesus face to face. I will be able to touch His nail-pierced hands. I will be able to ask Him all the questions I've wondered about. I will be able to thank Him for creating chocolate!

Mechelle Landaal

53

"I Can Only Imagine" always makes me stop and think. What will Heaven be like? How will I respond to being in the presence of the Almighty God? It is something I can't even imagine, because when I worship here on Earth I feel different ways. Sometimes, I want to jump and shout, other times I want to kneel before Him, and other times I just want to be quiet and rest in His presence. Sometimes there are tears, other times great happiness. So it's hard to imagine what it will be like to actually be standing before Him. I can't wait!

BONNIE SILVEUS

"I Can Only Imagine" is a beautiful song, but not one that struck me personally until I was at a MercyMe concert. Bart simply stopped singing a few bars into the song, pulled his monitor out of his ear and listened to the people singing.

We don't really know if there are streets of gold in Heaven. We don't know what angels will look like. But there will be singing, and it will be as communal and edifying and majestic as that moment.

Greg Batiansila

I am a former correctional officer at an Illinois county jail, where I was called upon to work the third shift one night. It was about 12:30 a.m., and most of the inmates had turned in except for one cellblock. Four inmates were still talking, and they asked if they could listen to the radio. The cellblock was dark. All the inmates were locked in with only their nightlights on. I placed the radio in the hallway and started to tune in a station, but finding one that everyone can compromise on is hard to do. All at once "I Can Only Imagine" was on the radio. All four of the inmates said, "leave it there!" I was shocked, but I left the radio on that song. A hush fell over the four inmates. You could have heard a pin drop. It really felt like the Spirit was moving in that cell that night. It was amazing.

I started to leave the cellblock and could hear the inmates discussing how that song moved them and where they stood in their lives. That song was the talk of the cellblock for a good four days. As a correctional officer, you try to forget a lot that happens in the jail, but this instance was different. It has really stuck in my mind.

Todd A. Fultz

FAITH ITSELF TAKES A LITTLE IMAGINATION—TO BELIEVE IN SOMETHING YOU CAN'T SEE, TO TRUST IN SOMETHING YOU CAN'T TOUCH, TO LISTEN TO THE VOICE OF A CREATOR YOU CAN'T PHYSICALLY HEAR, BUT WHO INSTEAD SPEAKS THROUGH NATURE, THROUGH THOSE AROUND US, AND THROUGH THE PAGES OF AN ANCIENT-BUT-TIMELESS BOOK. SOMETIMES IT CAN BE DIFFICULT TO TAKE THAT FIRST STEP, BUT FAITH WON'T GO UNREWARDED.

Then Jesus told him, "Because you have seen Me, you have believed;
blessed are those who have not seen
and yet have believed."
JOHN 20:29

I Can Only Imagine

"No eye has seen, no ear has heard,

no mind has conceived what God has prepared

for those who love Him."

1 Corinthians 2:9

Continue the *I Can Only Imagine* experience with other great music from MercyMe.

Undone
Spoken For
Almost There

www.mercyme.org
www.inorecords.com